LITTLE MISS
OVERSHARE

by Dan Zevin

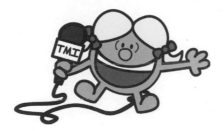

Illustrated by Dylan Klymenko

THREE RIV
NEW

D0619968

Little Miss Overshare was so excited, she jumped out of bed and ran straight to her roommate's room.

"Today is my birthday!" she shared. "It is the day my mother had a C-section because her cervix was not fully dilated and my head couldn't fit through her birth canal! Good morning!"

4:30 AM

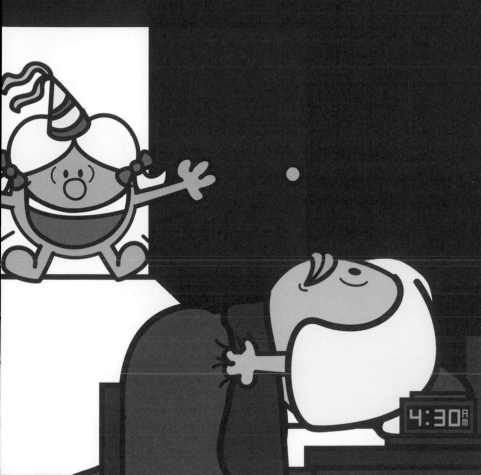

Miss Overshare waited for her roommate to sing her the "Happy Birthday" song.

But instead, she was silent.

My roommate is polite, sensed Miss Overshare. *She knows that interrupting is bad manners.*

4:34 AM

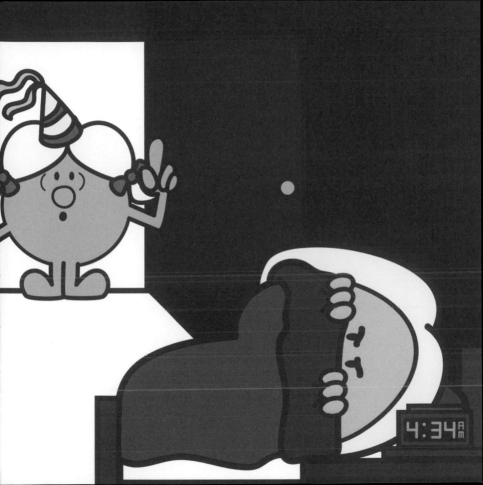

Well, Little Miss Overshare was polite, too!

She knew that *sharing* was *good* manners.

So she excused herself to go to the bathroom, explaining that she hadn't been able to move her bowels for three whole days.

"I think it's from the mozzarella!" she thoughtfully shared from the toilet seat.

Now her roommate wouldn't have to spend the rest of the day wondering!

On her walk to work, Little Miss Overshare cheerfully greeted the townspeople.

"Why, hello!" she called out to Mr. Butcher. "I am a vegetarian because I am morally opposed to eating anything that once had eyes!"

"Top of the morning to you!" she greeted Mr. Trash Man. "The reason I wash my hands every twelve minutes is because I have an obsessive compulsive disorder!"

"And how are *you* today?" she chirped to Mr. Donut Man. "I will have a vanilla swirl with no vanilla extract, please, since my father is an alcoholic."

When she finished her breakfast, she strolled to the bus stop.

There she met an old woman.

"Excuse me, dear," the old woman said. "Do you know how to get to Main Street?"

"Of course I do!" exclaimed Miss Overshare. "That is where my boyfriend lives!"

Miss Overshare moved closer and spoke right into the old woman's hearing aid.

"I'll tell you, at first I didn't think he'd be able to please me because of his erectile dysfunction, but ever since he started Cialis, it's like . . . you think *you* have trouble walking?"

Just then, the old woman did something silly.

She dropped dead of a heart attack.

"Oh my God!" Miss Overshare screamed.
"I have to write about this on my blog!"

Later, at work, she heard some colleagues chatting at the water cooler.

There was Little Miss Soccer Mom, who was always going on and on about carpooling. *TMI,* Miss Overshare thought.

And there was Mr. Meh, who told long-winded tales about the cute tricks his cat did each night. *STFU,* crossed her mind.

Still, she was thirsty, so she joined them.

"Would you like some water?" inquired Mr. Meh.

"Just an empty cup please," Miss Overshare replied. "I have to drink cranberry juice all week because of my urinary tract infection."

And then she showed them her urine sample.

At the end of the day, Miss Overshare made sure to let her supervisor know she'd have to leave right after the four o'clock meeting because she needed to pick up her dry cleaning by five to get to her parents' house in time for her birthday dinner even though she already brought that blouse to the lady, like three other times and the underarm stains were still there which was definitely the dry cleaner's fault, but it was also the deodorant's fault because no matter how many different brands she tried, she still had the same wetness issue, usually in her left armpit more than her right, but, look at this, right now they're *both* soaking, so that's why she got the name of dermatologist who specializes in perspiration disorders, except it's really hard to get an appointment with him because he's in the middle of a messy divorce and he spends most of his time in custody court, but why he would want those kids was beyond her anyway, since the boy is a kleptomaniac . . .

niversity College

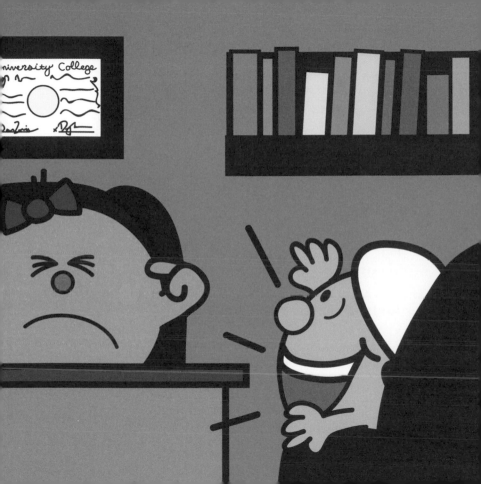

That evening, Little Miss Overshare celebrated her birthday with her family.

Her boyfriend couldn't come, but everyone understood when she said he had to be at his Gamblers Anonymous meeting.

So she sat by her favorite sister, Little Miss Undershare.

Her sister was so quiet; she never said a single word.

And can you guess why?

Of course you can!

Because she suffered from PTSD as the result of being raised in a dysfunctional family with no boundaries.

Just then, there was a festive sound.

Clink, clink, clink.

Her parents got up to make a toast!

"My menopause makes me overly sentimental," remarked Mama Overshare. "But it seems like only yesterday you were a freckle-faced fifteen-year-old, still wetting your bed."

Awww, that is so sweet, Little Miss Overshare thought.

Next, it was time for dear old dad, Papa Overshare.

When he opened his mouth, out came a great big belch!

"Guess I had a few too many birthday burritos!" he toasted his daughter.

"Not to mention a few too many birthday cocktails," Mama Overshare joshed.

That made them chuckle.

"Hey, if it wasn't for cocktails, we wouldn't even *have* a daughter to celebrate tonight. Cheers!"

Little Miss Overshare gave them a big hug.

By sharing the news that she was an unwanted child from a drunken hookup, her parents had given her the best birthday gift an oversharing girl could get.

A new topic to share with her book group!

When the party was over, Little Miss Overshare went to see her boyfriend, Mr. Tactless.

He was waiting in his apartment with her birthday gift.

It was a shiny engagement ring!

"This belonged to my great-grandmother," he said, looking deep into her eyes. "She gave it to me when she had her fingers amputated. Will you marry me?"

"Of course I will," she cooed. "I love you no matter what my therapist says."

And they stayed up all night long, calling everyone they knew to share their good news.

And also their plans for the mind-blowing sex they'd be having later that night to celebrate.

THREE RIVERS PRESS and the Tugboat design are registered trademarks of
Penguin Random House LLC.

Library of Congress Cataloging-in-Publication Data is available upon request.

ISBN 978-1-101-90445-9
eBook ISBN 978-1-101-90457-2

PRINTED IN CHINA

Illustrations by Dylan Klymenko
Cover design by Dylan Klymenko

10 9 8 7 6 5 4 3 2 1

First Edition